MY FIRST 30

MY FIRST 30

NADIRA PERSAUD

authorHOUSE®

AuthorHouse™
1663 Liberty Drive
Bloomington, IN 47403
www.authorhouse.com
Phone: 1-800-839-8640

Published by AuthorHouse   04/12/2012

ISBN: 978-1-4685-8546-9 (sc)
ISBN: 978-1-4685-8548-3 (e)

Library of Congress Control Number: 2012906824

I sit back and look at how I handled situations when I was younger. Either I was young or I just hadn't discovered pride yet. I was the most playful girl you could ever have imagined. I loved to laugh, and found humor in every situation possible. You couldn't even get me to be serious at a funeral. I remember happy days, I smiled, and sad days, I smiled. I walked in the rain as if the sun were out shining brightly, with my head held high. Nothing could have broken my spirit. I made friends everywhere I went, and was popular in school. They even voted me class clown in grammar school and in high school. I made everyone laugh, even myself.

Now I don't have a joke to save my life. I felt like my dream disappeared like the kid in me. I guess that's when life began for me.

A friend once told me that having faith and hope is not the only key to achieving what you want in life. You also have to fight for it. I thought to myself when she said that, and asked, "Why do I have to fight for what I want?"

I said to her, "Let me ask you a question now. Do you believe if you can't have what you want, then it's not worth having?"

We both laughed, not knowing how to answer our own questions. We will always have a million questions about life, but never have a million answers. Sometimes I feel some questions are better left unanswered, and we should just focus on the possible.

My name is Nadia. I was born in South America in a small country called Guyana. I have two beautiful parents that are still alive, yet separated. I come from a poor, uneducated family. My grandmother died when my mom was three years old, so she was raised by her sister. My mother was never given the opportunity to go to school as she had to work at the tender age of eight. My mother walked around with no shoes on her feet and barely any clothes on her back as she carried a basket of fruits on the top of her head to sell.

My mother said, "I loved watching the other kids go to school because they looked like they were having so much fun."

She said she would pray every night for a pair of shoes even though it would not change the fact that she still would be unable to go to school. She had to work because the family needed every penny they could get.

My father also came from a family of 12 siblings, but was not as poor as my mom. My dad was given the opportunity to go to school. It wasn't long after though that he had to drop out, leaving school at the age of 12 to help my grandfather who had just lost his leg in an accident.

My father and mother were introduced through an arranged marriage. My mother was 15. My father was 17. It's funny to think I was the product of an arranged marriage.

I remember asking my mom, "Did you love my dad?"

She said, "No. I had no idea who he was, but I had to do as my sister told me. As the years went by, I learned to love him."

My dad was a very abusive man towards my mother. I remember many nights, waking up and seeing blood all over my mother's face as my father would be kicking and punching her. I can recall one night my brother and I stood helpless, as he beat her with a four-by-four piece of wood. He had hit her so hard in the head that she fell unconscious, her head had burst open, and blood started gushing all over the place. I was six years of age at this time. All I could do was watch helplessly and cry as my brother held on to me in fear for our mother's life. I always wanted to know why my dad would come home and beat on my mom. I was confused. I didn't see her do anything wrong. I used to think he beat her because she didn't cook what he liked or clean the house the way he wanted it.

As I grew older, the beatings continued.

I asked my mom one day, "Why does dad beat you so much?"

She said to me, "He is jealous of me. He thinks I am having an affair when he goes out to work."

I knew she wasn't. She was right. My father was just a jealous man. He wanted her to stay in the house all day long. She was not even allowed to look out the window. My mom also was not allowed to work or go anywhere without my father. Even though my father was a mean man, he did love me and my brother Richard.

Richard is much older than I am, and had witnessed much more abuse than I did growing up. My brother holds my father responsible for the way his life turned out. He hated my dad because of the way he abused my mom. My brother was very intelligent. He was always at the top of his class, but he was a troubled kid. As he grew older, he himself had become abusive, lashing out at my father and anyone who got in his way. My brother handled every situation with violence. My mother feared that one day he would end up murdering someone. His temper was out of control. It's funny how the things our parents do can have such a great impact on our lives and to whom we become.

Despite what I witnessed, I was still a daddy's little girl. He used to spoil me rotten. I remember asking for a dog. Instead of buying me one, he bought me five. I even got a parrot that talked. I was his angel and in his eyes I did nothing wrong. As I grew older, I watched my father as he went from having nothing to becoming a wealthy man. We started to live like rich, spoiled kids. We had maids, one to cook our meals and one to wash our clothes. We even had security guards. I admired my father because he was a very hard-working man.

He made sure we had it all, but our lives didn't get easier just because money started coming in. My father wandered off a few times to his mistress. He was having an affair, but my mother had an idea. She followed him one day, crept up behind him as he was making out with his mistress. Just then, she picked up a glass bottle and cracked him in the head. She said he never cheated after that.

Living in a third world country, the laws sucked. If you had the money, you were the law, which meant that people paid their way out of everything, even murders. Men were allowed to beat their wives. Teachers were allowed to beat their students. I take no pride in my country or any country that condones abuse as the way to solve problems.

Coming from this environment, it was hard for my mother to leave my father. You see, they didn't believe in divorce in my country. Besides, where would she go? My father was all she knew, and he always handled the finances. She was just the housewife with no knowledge of the working world.

As my father's business grew, he made a name for himself by building one of the biggest houses in the village which created jealously amongst those around us. We had cars which people envied, and money that people wanted. For some reason though, my father wanted more. He wasn't satisfied with his riches. As a result, he got the idea that if he came to America, he could make twice the money he made in five years. So he decided to sell everything he owned, including his cars, trucks, and businesses, except for our house, and thought he was bringing us to America for a better life.

Well, that wasn't the case. When we came here, we lived in a basement apartment. My father couldn't find work. We struggled again. We were back to square one, starting from scratch. While his family members treated us like shit and guided us in the wrong direction, my father never gave up. He always said that his heart was made of steel, and he even went to get it tattooed on his arm. I started to believe it was true. Nothing could hold my dad back from reaching the top again, and I had faith in him. Four years later, we were once again on top, and this time in America living the American dream (but without American documents).

You see, we overstayed our welcome as we were had tourist visas. This made us illegal. Despite this fact, we continued to live normal lives until one day my mom saw a way to escape from under my father's grasp.

She said to me, "I am leaving your father now and you and your brother are old enough to understand. I was never happy, and I refuse to put up with any more abuse. It will feel like I am getting out of jail after 25 years."

I went to school that day because I didn't really think she would leave. My father was all she knew. She didn't even know how to read or write and didn't even have a dime to her name. For this reason, I wasn't worried. I thought she was just upset, and when I got back from school, she would still be there.

When I came home that day after school, to my dismay, my mother had lived up to her word and she was gone. She was like a fugitive on the run, leaving me and my brother behind. I was seventeen years old at the time and I was in my junior year of high school. As most teenagers, I had not a care in the world. I lived as each day came to me, irresponsibly and senseless as the last day. This is the day that my whole world turned for the worst.

I started to cry. All I could feel was hurt. I hated her with every part of my being for leaving me behind. My heart literally felt like it was breaking. This was my mother, and she left me. I remember telling myself that I would never forgive her, and that if I ever saw her again that I would not speak to her. How could she just up and leave? Didn't she think or care about what would happen to me if she left? How selfish she was to think of only herself. I wanted to know why she couldn't take me with her.

It took me one year to find the answers to my questions. I found out that my mother was living in Canada as a refugee. She could not afford to take us with her as she had no way to take care of me or my brother financially. She thought it was a better idea to leave us with our father, as he could provide us what we needed, which was food, clothing, and shelter. Little did she know that her idea became our worst nightmare.

My dad became an alcoholic right after she left, and spent most of his money trying to find her, not knowing that she was in a different country. My brother got tired of living with my father. Not only did my father become a drunk, he became abusive to us. As time went on, my brother also decided it was time for him to leave.

He said to me, "When I get myself situated, I will come back for you."

I was okay with that because I had a plan of my own.

I was in love with a guy named David Hutchinson. I met him in my sophomore year in high school. He was this calm, laid back guy, very friendly, and fit in with every crowd.

One day when I was at my locker, he passed by, took one look at me and said, "Damnnnn, you are sexy as hellll!"

My face blushed into the deepest shade of red imaginable as I smiled and thanked him. He walked back to my locker to where I was standing and handed me a piece of paper with his phone number.

He said, "Call me tonight around 10. I'll be by the phone waiting."

I said to myself that he would be waiting all night because I wasn't allowed to use the phone, especially to talk to boys, unless he was working for 911 as an operator, as this was the only number I was allowed to dial. Besides, we had only one phone in the house, and it was in my parents' room. There was no way in hell I could have called him.

I never got to call David that night.

When I saw him in school the next day, he asked, "What happened? I was by the phone waiting for your phone call."

"I lost your phone number," I told him.

He gave it to me again. I thought to myself: There goes one excuse. Let's see how many more I can come up with.

I watched him every day at lunch time and whenever he was in the hallways, chatting with his friends. He had the cutest dimples and I loved the way he laughed. All I kept thinking was that I needed to call him. I was dying to hear his voice over the phone. After hiding from him so that I wouldn't have to answer as to why I hadn't called him as of yet, I found the perfect opportunity.

When I didn't see him at school, I asked a friend where he was.

He said, "David was out sick."

To myself, I said, "Yes!"

This was my chance. I would call him from a payphone once I got out for lunch. So I did.

He answered and said, "Finally, you called."

We talked and he said that we had to hang out sometime.

"Do you cut classes?" I asked him. "It's the only time I can hang out because my parents are very strict."

School dismissed at 3:00, and I had to be home at 3:10 or else I would get an ass whooping if I was one minute later. I didn't tell him about the ass whooping part though. He said that okay, maybe we could go for a walk in the park.

One day we cut class together, and we walked, walked, and walked some more. I was tired. My little chicken legs were shaking with all that walking. I was a very petite girl, and weighed no more than 90 pounds.

"Can we sit?" I asked him.

"No, not in the park. We could get caught by my mom."

I didn't know he lived around the corner from the park. Anyway, we went into a building and sat on someone's staircase and continued to talk and talk. I was falling head over heels for him. I said to myself that I would marry him one day and get my papers.

It wasn't as easy as I pictured it to be. I had to put in a little bit more work than I thought. I signed up for an after-school program so I could get an extra hour to spend time with him. I also had competition with other girls that wanted to get his attention. However, I never gave up trying. I spent two years calling and chasing after him, until he realized I was never going to give up. He decided to give me a chance and finally asked me to be his girl.

My father found out that I was dating a man. A black man, to his surprise. My father was not at all happy with this information as it was against my culture to date or marry someone who is black. I had to marry within my own culture. My thought was that I was living in America, so that rule doesn't apply here. I didn't care. I was going to be with David with or without his approval. Well my father decided that he was not going to have a daughter who disgraced the family living in his home. He packed my things and threw them outside. I called David to let him know what happened, and he came by to pick me up with all my things.

After my father wasted all his money on getting drunk and not working, he gave up on searching for my mom, went back to live in South America, and left me here all alone. I stayed with David. He was living with his sister in the projects at the time. I was the only Indian girl in the entire projects. They had shootouts and killings almost every day. The building smelled of piss, and I had never seen so many roaches and rats in my life. I went from being rich to being beyond poor. I wasn't accustomed to this lifestyle.

I saw all different types of drugs and guns. It looked like these people were getting ready for war every day. This did not faze me because I adapted to the new environment. For a short time, I thought I could sell drugs too (just kidding . . . it was just a thought). I saw many crazy things. I thought this couldn't be real. They were killing themselves over fried chicken. I knew I had to get a job and get out of there soon. It doesn't matter how much you can adapt; it wasn't a safe place for anyone to live. Especially a girl like me.

I got a babysitting job paying $125 a week. At first, I had to take care of three kids and do laundry. Then, my boss asked me to do extra stuff, like vacuum, mop, clean the bathrooms, and help cook. I found myself doing everything. I wondered when she was going to ask me to sleep with her husband, as I thought that was the only thing left for me to do. One day, she asked if I knew how to iron. I said no as I knew what she was up to. She never gave me a raise for all the extra work I did. I decided to ask for one. She laughed and said she would give a $25 raise in six months if I continued the good work.

I felt like a slave, and was surely treated like one, too. She was the meanest woman I ever worked for and met in my entire life. Her name was Linda. She was from Africa. She was married to an African prince. They were rich but very cheap. She looked down on me because I was an illegal immigrant and I was young at the time. She spoke to me as if I were a servant. I couldn't eat when they had guests over. I had to wait until after the guests left to eat my dinner. I slept there on weekends to take care of the kids while she partied with her husband. I had to sleep in the same room as them because she said I wasn't allowed any privacy. Besides, if they needed anything in the middle of the night, I had to be right there. I prayed that she burn in hell every night for the way she treated me. I did love the kids and they loved me, too. I didn't have a choice anyway. I needed the money. Where else was I going to get a job? I had no green card.

After six months of dealing with this crazy bitch, I was ready to tell her suck a fat one. You see, I bumped into an old friend of my father's who asked me if I was working. He said he needed a receptionist from Monday to Friday, paying $250 a week. Oh boy. I felt like I hit the lottery when I heard what he said.

I told him, "Say no more. I want the job."

He replied, "Okay. You can start on Monday. Oh, and one more thing: I might need you to work every other Saturday, if that's okay with you."

I told him that I was okay with that because in my mind I was willing to work seven days a week.

After that conversation, I went on with my babysitting for the next couple of days, not saying anything to Linda as of yet. I was planning to finish up my last week with her and never go back, but little did I know I would be leaving sooner rather than later.

She had a visitor from London. She called the house phone, asking me if I could show her guest where everything was until she got home. I said I would. The woman started a conversation with me. She asked me about myself and told me about her. She was very sweet and polite. I wondered how she could be friends with this beast.

Little to my surprise, my boss came home and stood by the door, listening to our conversation without our knowledge. She barged into the room. Pissed off, she asked me why I was having a conversation with her guest. She told me I needed to leave the room right then and there. I turned to her and said, "You're a fucking bitch and I hope you burn in hell. I quit." This was one of the happiest days of my life as I watched the shocked look on her face as I left with a smile.

David was working in the nursing home doing dietary work and hustling on the side so we could get extra cash to move. I wasn't too happy with him hustling but he said that was the only way we would be able to save up fast enough to move.

One morning at work, I got a call from David's sister that he was arrested for drug possession. Immediately my reaction was that I wanted to go see him. Unfortunately, he was not allowed to have visitors until two weeks passed. As soon as the weeks went by, I went to pay him a visit.

During that visit he said, "They are going to give me three years and I need you to get me a lawyer." The very next day I went looking for an attorney.

The cheapest lawyer would cost me $2500. I had $1500 saved up. I decided to use that as a deposit so the lawyer could start working on the case. Two weeks later, the lawyer contacted me and said that David wouldn't be getting out soon.

I asked, "How much jail time are we talking about?"

The lawyer said, "A minimum of six months."

At that time, six months seemed like a lifetime. I visited David every Wednesday for the next six months. I never missed a visit. Rain, snow, even being without money, I still made it there. I was only allowed thirty minute visits. I used to love all the little pictures and poems he would do for me. We always looked forward to these visits. Before we knew it, the day of his release came. We held on to each other like two leeches.

Later on that evening, he said, "I drew something for you but you have to close your eyes." He got on one knee and said, "Open your eyes." It was a drawing of Alvin and the Chipmunks. Alvin was holding a ring saying, "Will you marry me?"

I said, "Yes, but eventually I will need a real ring. I can't walk around with this drawing and tell people that this is my ring."

He laughed and said, "You know I will."

I saw this as the perfect time to let him know about my situation. I told him I needed to get married right away in order to stay in this country because I was illegal.

He looked at me and said, "I would watch you every Wednesday as you would walk over that bridge to come see me and you never missed a day because of you I'm not doing three years in jail. So my question to you is tomorrow too soon?"

We got married August 2, 2004. I filed my papers that very same year. We got our own little one-bedroom apartment away from the projects. Things were starting to look up. One year later, I got pregnant. I gained only ten pounds during the entire pregnancy.

I kept my marriage and pregnancy a secret from my mom. I knew it would kill her to know I married a black man, nevertheless having his baby. I wasn't ready to give her a heart attack as of yet. I spent many months debating whether to keep the baby or not until I realized I was six months too late and had no choice.

I called my mom and told her that I got married and was pregnant. My mother screamed so loud

I swear I could have heard her from Canada. She started to cry. She questioned how I could disgrace the family like this. She told me that I needed to get rid of the baby or forget I have a mother. I told her it was too late for that because I was six months pregnant.

I could've sworn I was killing my mother slowly. I could tell it in her voice.

She said, "Well, when the baby is born, take it to an adoption agency. Give it away. If you don't do as I tell you, don't ever call my phone again." She hung up on me.

I wanted to drive my car into a pole and kill myself. It hurt to hear what my mother just told me. Here, I was falling in love with this unborn baby but I couldn't keep it. I told my husband everything that my mother said.

He hugged me so tight. Then he went on and said, "We are not giving up our baby. Your mother is just angry at the moment. She will get over it. Just give her some time."

I went into labor March 17th. I was scared with no one by my side but my husband. How I wished my mom could've been there to share this special moment with me.

I told my husband how I felt. He left the room. He called my mom to tell her I was going into labor. From then on, I remembered she called the phone every ten minutes. David spoke to her. He didn't want her to upset me anymore.

All he said to me was, "Your mom is very worried about you."

The baby finally got here. David called my mom right away so she could hear her grandbaby cry. My mom asked to speak to me.

I said, "Hello."

All I could hear was her crying.

Through her tears, she said, "I know I said some hurtful things. I want you to keep the baby. I will do whatever I can to help you with her. Now please put the phone by my grandbaby's ear so I can hear her cry. Oh, I got the perfect name for her, let's call her Reanna."

Now, my mother can't live or breathe without Reanna. Everything is for her grandbaby.

After giving birth, I soon felt sick. The doctor who delivered Reanna had left a piece of placenta inside of me which caused me to bleed. I knew something wasn't right. I went to the hospital one week after giving birth. The doctor gave me a check-up, told me that everything looked fine, and that it was normal to bleed after having a baby, sometimes up to two weeks. I went back home to take a nap. I was starting to feel weak. I woke up in a puddle of blood. I got myself cleaned up, thinking that this was not normal. I had no appetite. I could hardly stand. I was about half dead when my husband found me. I lost so much blood that you would've thought you were looking at a crime scene. He called 911 right away.

I was rushed to the hospital. I remember my eyes were closing in on me. I could only hear my husband talking to the doctor. The doctor asked him to sign a paper so I could be rushed into surgery before I died. I felt my husband hold my hand. He gently whispered into my ear that he was scared and asked me not to die. It was all I could remember.

I woke up the next day in the recovery room. I couldn't believe I was alive. I guess God wasn't ready for me. I was released from the hospital, and couldn't wait to get home to see my daughter, thinking that life was only going to get better from now on.

I thought I had the perfect family. I was young and naïve. There were many nights that I spent up as my husband didn't come home. When he did get home, he used pathetic excuses, but I believed and forgave him anyway. I wondered to myself how many times he was going to use the excuse that he fell asleep at his brother's house. It was difficult to find out if he was lying as his brother would cover for him.

Many females approached me and said they were sleeping with him. When confronted with this information, his defense would be that these other females were jealous of what we had. Once again, I believed. Until one day, I realized I couldn't keep living like this. I couldn't keep on praying that he would come home every night. It got so bad that I had many sleepless nights, staying up worrying if he was okay.

My husband had lost his job. When he told me he was going to work, he was hanging out with strippers and whores. Although he was doing this,

I still helped him out. I tried getting him a job with people with whom I had connections, but first he had to take a drug test. I told my friend that it wouldn't be a problem. My asshole of a husband went to take the drug test, as if he never did drugs a day in his life, with so much self-assurance that it gave me confidence that he wasn't doing drugs. Then I received a phone call and found out my husband tested positive for PCP. I wanted to have a heart attack. When I confronted him, he said, "I did that a long time ago. I am surprised it is still in my system." If only his nose grew when he lied, it could have reached China.

This happened around Christmas. On December 31, my husband told me that he was going to the store to buy some champagne as we could ring in the New Year. I replied okay. He left and never returned. I got on my knees that night and asked God for the courage to leave him as I cried myself to sleep, holding my daughter in my arms. The next day I got an even more shocking phone call from his best friend who said he needed to talk to me. I left work early that day as I needed to know what was so important.

He said, "Nadia, I can't lie to you anymore. David has been cheating on you. Now he is sleeping with my girlfriend. I caught them together in the bathroom last night. I'm sorry. You are a very sweet girl. You can do much better. You need to leave him."

Sitting there in shock, I thought that if you would cut my wrists, you wouldn't find any blood. I felt dead inside. With that being said to me, I knew this was my sign from God to break free.

I started to look for a new apartment right away. God was so great. I found one that same week. My best friend came over with her husband's truck, and I took all that I needed and moved that very same day. This all happened within a week. I was ready for a change. I had had enough.

I heard from my neighbor that he came home the following week to work things out and was surprised to find an empty house. He began to call my phone, harassing me. I was in a state of shock when he arrived at my workplace. I worked very far away at that time. I asked him how he got there. He replied that he took two buses and a train. I told him that he needed to leave because I was going to call the police. He said that if I called the cops, he would tell my boss that I was stealing money and make me lose my job. I asked him why he would tell such a nasty lie as I never stole shit, and he knew this. Then I asked if he thought that he would be back with me by telling things that were not true, and he left off in a furious state.

He was searching for where I lived for the past three months and could not locate me. For this reason, he started to follow me home from work. All he needed to know was where I lived. The next day, I came home from work to find him in my apartment, with a knife in his hand. He looked as if he hadn't slept in months and lost about fifty pounds. He appeared truly enraged. At that point, I didn't care. He deserved to suffer after all he had put me through. As they say, you don't know what you have until you lose it.

I asked him how he got into my home. He told me that he climbed up the fire escape and came in through the bathroom window. I turned so pale, you would have thought you were looking at a dead person. As I turned around to run out the door, he picked up a chair and threw it at me. I fell and hit my head on the door. Then he grabbed me, dragged me back into the house, locked the door, and started to cry. He said he was sorry and wanted to talk. He begged for another chance, saying that he had changed. I thought to myself, "Yeah, right. You turned into a fucking psychopath."

I had heard this a million times before. I told him that he needed to leave and that I wanted nothing to do with him.

Although I thought he would leave, things just got worse. He put a knife to my throat and said, "I'm not going anywhere. I'll stay here until we work things out." My phone was in my pocket. I just had to find a way to use it. He sat right next to me on the bed, talking and talking. All I could think was, "How did my life end up like this? Is this how I'm going to die? Is this the man I once loved and couldn't picture my life without?"

I asked if I could use the bathroom. He said yes. He grabbed me by the arm and walked me to the bathroom.

I asked him to close the door and he said, "No. You can use the bathroom in front of me."

I said, "Okay."

Then I thought to myself that Plan A didn't work. He took me back to the room, and I told him to go to the kitchen to get me some water. All of a sudden, my phone began to ring. I answered as quickly as possible. It was my best friend calling to say hello.

As fast as I could, I said, "David is here and I need help."

She asked, "Do you need me to call the police?"

I said, "Yes, please hurry."

He heard, and grabbed the phone, breaking it into two pieces. I said to myself, "I'm fucked."

Now I was scared. I had never seen my husband like this before. He was furious. He told me to sit down. He told me that if I tried to get up, he would kill me.

"Holy shit, "I thought to myself. "He's gone mad."

I was trying to be brave despite my fear. I told him that he could kill me as I wasn't scared. I started hitting him in the face. He got so mad and slammed me on the bed and started to choke me. Thank God, the cops knocked on the door just then.

He told me to go to the door to tell them to leave and that everything is okay inside. The officer said he needed to look at me before he left. I opened the door. From the look on my face, he knew I wasn't fine.

One officer took me to the side and asked me, "Honey, are you okay?"

I said, "No. My husband is trying to kill me."

The officer arrested him on the spot. I went down to the precinct and filed a restraining order.

I continued with my regular routine after the incident. Despite everything my husband had done to me, I was feeling guilty that he was sitting behind bars. Never did I expect or want this situation to get out of control like this. How can a man destroy me physically, mentally, and emotionally, and yet I still love him unconditionally? Was I crazy, or was this what love did to people? I asked myself. I wanted him to change because deep down in my heart, I still had hope for us, but I refused to be unhappy.

On September 19th, I was sitting at my desk at work typing, and looked up and spotted this handsome guy with beautiful eyes. He was black with Chinese eyes. I couldn't help but stare. He caught me staring, and he smiled, and so did I. As I continued to type, I had to take one more look again. As I lifted my head up, he was gone, so I went back to my typing, and all of a sudden, I heard a voice say, "Hello."

When I looked up, there he was, smiling.

My heart started beating, and I said, "Hello."

He said, "Can I have your number?"

I quickly said, "Yes," real loud out of nervousness.

He laughed and said, "My name is Mike by the way."

Since I'm a little deaf, he had to repeat his name about four times to me. That was an awkward moment for me. We exchanged numbers, and he left. We began to talk that very first night.

He had moved up here from South Carolina to pursue his dream in music, and was hired by one of the biggest record labels known around the world, Def Jam. He did a little bit of everything. He rapped, produced, recorded, and wrote. Since he wasn't from New Jersey, and only been living here for six months, I decided to give him a little tour. This would be our first date. He enjoyed all the sightseeing. I enjoyed looking at him. He said that was the first time leaving the house since he'd been living up here, and that ours was the best first date he'd ever had.

As the time passed, we got closer and more attached. It was starting to get serious. I was having all these feelings I hadn't felt in eight years. I wondered to myself if it was love. It sure felt like it. We acted like it, and it had only been three months. I could name twenty things I loved about him, and one thing I hated. What were the odds of me walking away from something so good?

Well, my husband was released from jail after doing seven months, and was up to his old tricks again. It was obvious that jail had served no purpose to him. I was in my deep sleep one night and I don't know what made me open my eyes, but I found my husband over me, very angry and furious. He was about to strangle me.

I jumped up, and he said, "You've been cheating on me while I was in jail."

With my cell phone in his hand, he began to read all the text messages that Mike and I had sent to each other . . . and trust me, there was some nasty stuff in those text messages that made him so mad that he looked like the Devil had taken over his body; and I was praying for Jesus to take over mine.

He looked at me with tears in his eyes, and asked, "How can you do this to me? I would give up my life for you. I feel like killing you and killing myself right now. If I can't have you, no one can."

I was in shock to know that he'd gotten into my house, so my first question to him was, "How the hell did you get into my house this time?"

I had arranged for a friend to come to my house, secure the windows, and put an extra deadbolt on my door because I knew he was being released from jail. I didn't know whom I wanted to kill more: my friend who did a sloppy job in securing the place, or my husband who kept breaking in. At the time, my co-worker had moved into the apartment next to me, and we became very close. So she knew about my situation, and she saw when he broke into my apartment, but she didn't have a phone to call the cops. My husband and I started to argue and fight. He got so angry at me that he started to choke me, and I was screaming. But one thing he'd forgotten to do was lock the door on his way into the house. My co-worker heard the argument, and she came rushing in. She saw him on top of me, and told him that he needed to get off me, because she'd just called the cops, and they were on their way.

He got off of me, took my phone and fled the apartment, saying to my friend, "You need to mind your fucking business before I come after you next."

I asked my friend, "Did you really call the cops?"

She said, "No, I just said that so he would leave."

And I asked, "What if he had killed us both before he left?" I knew it was a serious situation, but I still found the humor in it.

She said, "Oh, I didn't think about that."

But I was very grateful she'd saved me.

I knew this was not going to get better. I had to move again. Since he took my phone, I had no way of getting in contact with Mike, but my husband sure as hell did. When I got to work the next day, I called Mike to let him know what had happened, and that I didn't have my phone anymore.

He said to me, "I figured that. Your husband called me about twenty times, and informed me to stay the hell away from you or else he would kill me."

I began to look for a new place once more to get away from this madman of a husband. I would wake up every day to all my tires flattened, and him calling me to tell me it wasn't over. I didn't want to take the risk of having Mike over the house because I didn't know if my husband was spying on me. To prevent waking up to flat tires every morning, I spent some nights at Mike's house.

I informed my mother-in-law of what David was doing. She asked me to help her to get him to come down to South Carolina. We both thought it was a good idea for him. He needed some time to think and relax his mind. I just wanted him to get the hell away from me before he caused more damage. Besides, his mother was worried sick about what he might do next. I was getting 73 missed calls a day with threats from my husband. I decided to answer him one day.

I said to him, "I'll give you one more chance under one condition: If you go stay with your mother for a few months and get yourself together."

He replied, "Will you be coming with me?"

"I'll meet you down there," I said. "You can take the baby with you and go spend some time with your mother."

He was so happy to hear that I said he could take our daughter, because he knew my daughter was my world. I knew that was one of the reasons that he would go because I agreed to let him take our child. I know some of you may judge me and ask why I trusted him with my child if he was abusive to me. You see, he wasn't a good husband, or had no idea what a husband's role should be. But he was a wonderful father. Our daughter was his world, too. I knew that if I let him take her, she might help him see that he had something to live for. With that being said, he agreed to go to South Carolina and stay with his mom for a while. Little did he know though that his mother had bought him a one-way ticket and had no intention of letting him come back to New Jersey. He and my daughter left to South Carolina, and I continued my regular routine of work and seeing Mike.

It was getting close to the holiday season. Mike was going home to visit his grandparents who had taken care of him after the death of his mother. He had never known his father, so his grandparents were everything to him. Since they lived in South Carolina, I said to myself, "What a coincidence. What a small world."

He was from the same general area in which my husband was staying. I thought it was a good idea for us both to drive there because I wanted to see my daughter. I missed her dearly. Although I had to come face-to-face with my husband, I didn't really care. All I could think about was seeing my daughter.

We set off for South Carolina together. When we arrived at Mike's grandparents' house, he said to me, "I never brought a girl home that I didn't love, and I've only brought a girl home once. So I would like for you to meet my grandparents."

I was touched, nervous, scared, sweating, but it was all for a good reason. I met his grandparents, and oh boy, I felt as if I were on trial with his grandmother. But his grandfather was awesome. He liked me from the moment he met me. I stayed for about an hour and as I was about to leave, Mike said to me, "I know you will be around your husband. I can't talk to you as much as I want to, but just remember that I love you."

I felt that I'd waited all my life to hear those words. It was a moment that I wanted to last forever. I was falling in love again.

He also said to me, "You were with your husband for many years. I know you still love him. Please don't cheat on me because I'm giving you my heart."

I looked at him and said, "I would be a fool if I did."

I set off to my husband's house which was about an hour and a half away from Mike's grandparents' house. My husband had no idea I was coming, only his mother. When I arrived, he wasn't home.

His mother greeted me and said, "David isn't staying here. He's staying at his grandfather's house, so he won't be bothering you. You are welcome to stay as long as you like."

This is too good to be true, I said to myself, but knowing my husband, the minute he knew I was around, he would put on a cape and fly to me. Sure enough, he did. The first question he asked me was: "Where is he?"

I asked, "Who?"

He said, "Mike. I know you didn't drive all this way by yourself."

I could have sworn there was pee dripping down my legs. He wasn't dumb after all, I said to myself. But I kept my cool, and said, "You are crazy. Why would I come down here with Mike? I haven't seen or heard from him since you told him you were going to kill him if he didn't stay away from me."

I was surprised he believed my story, but then again, I could win an Oscar for my acting, or I should say lying.

Seeing my husband was very hard. I was still in love with him. I never hated him. I just hated the things he'd done while we were together. In the middle of our conversation, his grandfather called, and my husband said he had to leave. He assured me that he was going back home with me and that he was very happy I came to work things out. He finally thought he was getting his family back. All I could think in my head was, "What have I done?"

I wasn't too sure that I was ready to take him back because I was now falling in love with Mike. I lay on the bed for about four hours thinking, until my head hurt. I tried to figure out who was the better choice for me. I thought about such things as, who loved me more, who I loved more, who I had fun with, and who truly made me happy. At the same time, I wanted to know who loved me more as well. All I knew was that for eight years, I was with my husband. I can't remember how many of those years I was happy. Then there was Mike who made me feel happy every day since I'd met him. Mike gave me a totally different feeling about love, a feeling I'd never felt in my whole life. Not even with my husband. I was so confused that I turned to God and asked him to give me a sign. Who should I be with?

The next day I got up and took my daughter to the aquarium to spend some time with her. I needed more time to think. When I got back to the house, my husband was there waiting for me. I'd seen that look on his face before.

I said to myself, "That was the look he gave me when he was about to strangle me to death."

He looked at me, and asked, "Where were you?"

I said, "I went to the aquarium to spend some time with Reanna."

He said, "You're lying. I called you about fifteen times, and your phone went straight to voicemail."

I said, "I never received any calls. My phone had no service."

He didn't believe me. He said, "I know you went to see Mike."

He grabbed me by my hair and called me a liar, and was about to hit me in my face.

Just then, his mother jumped in the middle and stopped him. She said, "Nadia, go to my house and wait for me. And you, David, will stay here at your grandfather's house. Don't come to my house until Nadia leaves. If I ever see you raise your hand again to her, I will chop it off myself."

I got in to my car and drove to my mother in law's house. When I got there, I started to pack my things.

As I was packing, I said to God, "I guess this was your sign. He hasn't changed. My husband is even more violent now."

I waited for my mother-in-law to get home. We sat down and talked. I asked her to keep my daughter in her care until I could get back on my feet.

She said, "Whatever you need help with, I'm here for you. I consider you as my daughter and I only want the best for you and my grandbaby. For my son, he needs help. I don't advise you to take him back if he is this abusive."

I grabbed my things. I kissed my daughter and said to her, "I'll be back for you real soon."

I got in my car and left. I remember crying for two hours straight. Leaving my daughter behind was the hardest thing I'd ever had to do in my life. I had to do it. Most people would say they could never leave their child behind, but I honestly had no choice. I had no family to turn to for help. I couldn't afford a babysitter. I didn't qualify for any public assistance, since I didn't have my papers at that time. With my daughter's grandmother, I was guaranteed that my daughter was safe and secure. Her grandmother loved and spoiled her rotten. I was confident with my decision.

I finally made it to Mike's grandparents' house to pick him up so that we could head back to Jersey. We talked and talked for twelve hours straight. I told him everything that happened. He told me not to worry about anything. He'd be there for me for whatever I needed. He made me feel so safe. I looked at him and thought to myself, "I feel like I found the man of my dreams." It's hard to find someone to understand you when you can barely understand yourself. Deep down inside, I knew I had a lot more to learn about love. I enjoyed our conversation. We laughed. We even argued. Those arguments didn't last longer than ten minutes, though, and we were back in love again. I couldn't have been happier with my decision. This was what I'd always wanted: A man to love me as much as I loved him. Well, at least, this was what I thought.

You see, this is what happened. When we got back to New Jersey, I noticed more arguments were starting. We started to fight over little things. Jealousy got the best of both of us. He had a little more to hide than I thought. Let me sum it up for you: Once upon a time there was a boy and girl in love, and then a hoe came along. The End.

Mike and I got into heated arguments. This one was the worst. As we were driving, he pulled over to run into the store to get something to drink. His phone rang and I answered it. I said, "Hello" twice, and then a female responded, "Why are you answering Mike's phone?"

I said, "Well, you nosy bitch, if you must ask, I have every right to answer his phone, because I'm his girlfriend . . . and can I help you?"

She said to me, "Whoever this is, you need to stop playing on his phone and hang up." When he got into the car, I was so angry. I punched him in the face. His head hit the glass window.

He said, "What the hell is wrong with you? I got you something to drink, too."

I said, "No, you asshole. Who is this?" showing him the cell phone.

"Oh, she's nobody. That girl is crazy, and won't stop calling my phone. And if you believe anything she said, you're crazy, too."

I'm not going to lie. I did believe he was telling me the truth. I started to run through his phone constantly, and the more I did, the more I found out. He was talking to at least five girls and the conversation was all sexual. I didn't trust him, but I didn't have the heart to walk away. Things were changing between us. It was clear to see that we were headed to a dead end. I still held on.

After the argument about all the females in his phone, we hadn't spoken for two weeks. He sent me a message on a Monday morning, saying he missed me and wasn't going anywhere. My face lit up and my heart was happy. Later on that evening, I decided to pay him a surprise visit.

When I got to the house, I rang the bell. His roommate came to the glass door and said, "Hold on."

I said to him, "Open the door."

He said, "Hold on, let me get Mike first."

Right then and there, I knew something was going on. They always opened the door for me.

Mike called my phone and said, "What are you doing here? You need to go home."

In shock, I said, "No. I'm not going anywhere until you come down and talk to me or I'm going to break this door down."

By then, I figured he had a girl in the house.

I saw his room light come on. I yelled through his window, "I know you have a bitch in your house."

After I said that, a female came to the window asking me who I was.

"I'm his girlfriend that he's been with for two years," I answered. "Who the hell are you?"

She replied, "I'm his girlfriend, too."

I turned ten different shades of red. I felt as if the devil had taken over my body. I started kicking the door and cursing at the top of my lungs.

"Open this door or I'm going to kill you!"

It was a glass door. I could see him pacing back and forth, smoking cigarette after cigarette. The girl wouldn't come downstairs. She stayed in the room, looking at me through the window, scared. Oh, how badly I wanted to get into that house and get my hands on him.

I found a brick at the side of the house and when I was about to break the glass door, a neighbor came out and said, "I just called the cops. You are disturbing the peace."

Two minutes later, the cops came and asked me a few questions.

I explained my story to them. The officer told me I was going to have to leave or they were going to arrest me. I got into my car in shock, praying to wake up from this nightmare, asking God to please let this be a dream. Here I am with evidence in front of me, and I still couldn't believe what I was seeing. How can he look me in the face and say that he loved me and would never leave me, but meanwhile, here I was, the woman he loved, on the other side of the door?

It sure as hell wasn't a dream. Around nine the next morning, he called. I answered the phone and said, "You have some nerve calling my phone."

He said, "Please don't hang up on me, I'm begging you. I am a dog for what I did, and I am so sorry. Please, let's work this out. She means nothing to me."

I asked him if he was on crack. I asked him if he didn't realize what went on last night. I think I invented a curse word for every letter in the alphabet. I called him every name I could think of off the top of my head. I didn't want to hear anything he had to say. I decided to hang up the phone. It was time to walk away. He didn't deserve me. I thought it would be as easy as it was with my eight year relationship. Boy was I wrong. The pain in my heart was unbearable. The tears were unstoppable. I saw all the reasons he began to cheat. The more his career grew, the more celebrities he met, the more he was tempted. A lot of females were interested in him, but for all the wrong reasons. I was the only girl who treated him differently. I wasn't afraid to walk away when I had enough. He thought I would never leave.

I haven't seen him since that night he got caught, although he tried to reach out to me many times. I never responded. It had been two years since the whole incident. Then, one evening I got a call from him.

I answered the phone. He said, "Do you know who this is?" I said, "Yes, this is the dick that cheated on me two years ago," and laughed.

He laughed in return.

I said, "What is this phone call about?"

At this point, I was way over the situation. I could care less what he had to say, but I had a motto: I like to play dumb to see how far a man will go before they fuck up. I don't look for closure. It serves no purpose in my book. I'm a simple yes-or-no girl. I don't believe in ifs or buts. I forgive easily because I have short term memory. I don't dig too deep because I'm not looking for skeletons. I believe you can find the truth in every lie.

He said to me, "It's been two years since we broke up, and I still can't stop thinking about you. I really did love you, Nadia, and I'm sorry for everything that happened, and I was wondering, could we go out to dinner some night, if that is okay with you?"

I said it wouldn't be a problem, but I don't like to visit my past. You see, my cousin told me that Mike was still with the girl that he cheated on me with, and she was now pregnant. He and I talked for a few minutes, and he started to tell me he missed the sex, and if there was any way we could have sex again.

I asked him, "Are you single?"

He said, "Yeah."

I laughed and I said, "It was nice talking to you, and by the way, congratulations on becoming a father." I hung up the phone, not waiting for a response, and I said to myself, "Some people will never change."

As I was on my way home from doing some errands one day, I pulled into my driveway and saw the UPS guy ringing the doorbell with a package in his hands. I couldn't see his face.

As I was walking toward him, I said, "Who is the package for?"

When he turned around, I thought I was looking at an angel. With a smile on his face, he said, "I'm looking for Miss Williams."

I said, "It's the people who live upstairs."

He said, "Would you like to sign for this package?"

I said, "No thank you. I don't want to sign for anything that doesn't belong to me."

This guy was tall, well-built, and had some beautiful hazel eyes, and a smile to die for. I was thinking to myself: Was this what love at first sight felt like? As he was talking to me, I looked at his finger to see if there was a wedding ring, and his finger was in the clear.

As he was walking away, I had to get his attention, so I said, "I'm expecting a package. Do you have anything for me?"

He said no. Well, of course he didn't, because I was lying.

Second question: "Will you be delivering tomorrow as well?"

He said yes, that he delivered every day.

I said, "Okay," and he left.

I tried checking my mail around the same time he made his last delivery, to ask more questions about my fake package, but I had no luck to ever catch him. I was online one day and decided to order a bathing suit and have it UPSed to me. Now I finally had something to be delivered. I got my tracking number and all the other information

I needed, such as when and what time I should expect my package. Now I just had to sit back and wait. The day of the delivery, I decided to look a little extra nice. I wore a low-cut shirt to show some cleavage. I think it was showing too much cleavage. Any lower and my nipple would have popped out.

This was definitely going to get his attention. My hair and makeup were done as well. I decided to sit on my porch and wait. The UPS truck pulled up and it wasn't him. It was some other guy with my package. He said, "I have a package for a Nadira Persaud. Is that you?"

I said, "No, I don't live here. I'm just waiting for someone."

He rang the bell, and of course, no one came to the door, because the person who lived there was sitting right next to him.

So I said, "I've never seen you before. I live across the street. What happened to the other delivery guy?"

"The younger gentleman?" he asked. "He will be back tomorrow."

The delivery man asked me if I wouldn't mind signing for the package, and I said no, that I didn't want to be responsible for anyone's stuff. I wanted to laugh at the same time. This was the most ridiculous thing I had ever done.

I said to him, "You will have to try again tomorrow."

In my head, I couldn't wait for tomorrow to come.

Once again, I got dressed and waited.

Finally, the man I'd been waiting for . . . and he was delivering my package. I had a smile from ear to ear.

He said, "You look very happy to see your package. I know you've been waiting for it for a long time now."

What I wanted to say was, "That's not the only package I'd like to see."

But what I actually ended up saying was, "Actually, no. I couldn't wait to see you again."

He blushed as he smiled, and said, "Oh really? I don't want your boyfriend coming outside and beating me up for hitting on you."

I said, "I don't see anyone coming outside, so that must mean I don't have a boyfriend."

We both giggled and blushed.

He said, "My name is Shawn, by the way."

I said, "Okay, Shawn. Take my number down, and maybe we can grab lunch sometime."

We exchanged phone numbers. He called me that evening. We talked for about three hours. We'd talk more and more every day. I wanted to know everything about him. He wanted to know everything about me. I went outside every chance I got to get a glimpse of him as he made his deliveries. He would stop to give me a quick hug and a kiss on the cheek.

He asked me one night, "How would you like your first date to be?"

I said, "I've never had a guy bring me flowers on a date before, so that would be nice. And I'd like to go for a walk on the beach."

"I can do roses," he said, "but I'm not too sure about the walk on the beach. This is Jersey City, remember? If you're not doing anything this weekend, let's go out. Is Friday okay with you?"

I answered, "Yes."

He said, "I'll pick you up around seven," and he did. With flowers.

I asked him, "Where are we going?"

He said it was a surprise. We were driving for about forty minutes now. All I saw were bushes and trees. I said to myself, "Oh my God, he's about to cut me up into pieces and throw me in the bushes."

I had to text one of my friends, that I was on a date with a UPS guy just in case I went missing.

Anyway, he took me to this restaurant on a hill. It was so beautiful. The view was amazing. The restaurant had no tables or chairs. We sat on the floor and ate dinner. I felt like I was having dinner in China.

At one point, I asked him, "Why is a handsome guy like you single with no kids?"

He said, "I've been in the army for eight years, and I just got back from Iraq ten months ago, then I started working for UPS. But I just signed back up again because I love the army."

I said to myself, "Isn't this a bitch, when I thought I'd found Mr. Right, and now he's going away to the army."

"So how long do I have with you before you leave?" I asked.

He said, "I have two more months, and this is the reason that I haven't been dating or wanted to get involved with anyone."

All I could say to that was, "Well then, let's make this the best two months you've ever had."

I asked him, "Is there anything you would like to do before going back to the army?"

He said, "Yeah. I'm doing it now. I'm having dinner with the most beautiful girl ever."

My heart melted. We spent every moment possible with each other after that, and talked each chance we got.

He called me one afternoon and said, "Get dressed and come outside." I went outside. He was sitting on my porch with roses.

He said, "Let's go for a drive."

I knew something was wrong.

He looked at me, and said, "I only have two days left, Nadia. I'm leaving on Monday. I was called in earlier."

I wanted to stand on top of a mountain and scream at the top of my lungs just to hear my pain echo until it faded away. That night he took me to the beach.

We sat in the sand and he looked at me and said, "Don't look so sad. We will keep in touch. I promise I will write you every possible moment I get."

I told him, "Let's make this night memorable. I've never had sex on the beach before."

He smiled and said, "Me neither."

We found a quiet spot away from any light or people, and I'll leave the rest to your imagination.

The day before he left, I cooked him dinner. Over dinner, I asked him to promise me that he would keep in touch.

He said, "I promise. But I think we should also make this last day memorable, too."

I said, "I think you are just using this going-away crap just to sleep with me."

He laughed and said, "Is it working?"

I replied, "Let's go to the room and find out."

We said our goodbyes that night, and I didn't hear from him. Three weeks later, he wrote to tell me he was in Baghdad and everything was fine.

And every time it wasn't, he would picture my smile.

He said, "I'll write to you when I get settled in. They're moving me again."

I didn't hear from him until six months later.

He wrote, "Hey, Nadia. Sorry for not writing, but it's crazy over here. You wouldn't begin to understand. I'm on a battlefield. I hear gunshots all day long. It's starting to sound normal to me. I've been very depressed. I lost my close friend three months ago and another one two weeks ago in an explosion right in front of me. I'm not going to lie. I was very scared."

He went on talking about the war. I guess he needed to vent, so he did it in the letter.

At the end of the letter, he said, "I won't ask you to wait for me because that would be selfish. Besides, it would be like waiting for a dead man to come back alive."

This was the last time I ever heard from him. It's been one year now, and still nothing. Sometimes I sit on my porch and wait for the UPS truck to pull up, hoping he will jump out, and then I realize that only happens in movies. He is just a memory to me now . . . a good memory, and that's the way I want to keep it.

Within that year, I met a cop. One afternoon, I was on my way to return some movies. As I was driving and not paying attention, there was a cop in his car staring right at me. As I caught myself, I dropped my phone as fast as possible. I saw in my rear view mirror as he turned his car around. Before I knew it, he pulled me over to the side of the road. He got out of his car. I totally forgot I wasn't wearing my seatbelt.

He said to me, "You should be wearing your seatbelt. You should also know that there is a fine for using your cell phone while driving."

In a rage, I got out of my car, saying to him, "Why don't you go stop crime instead of worrying about something as silly as a stupid seatbelt? You are not giving me a ticket."

What the fuck was I thinking saying this to a cop?

I guess I was angry because of the four tickets I received in the last month for running red lights and speeding. I had reasons to be tired of these cops.

He said smiling, "Calm down. I am not giving you a ticket. Oh boy, you got a mouth on you. I have every right to give you a ticket because I was watching you on your cell phone and without your seatbelt. I will give you a warning instead. And my phone number. Maybe I can take you out and we can get to know each other."

I smiled back. Then I replied, "Is this how you pick up the girls?"

He laughed and said, "No, this is my first time even trying something like this. My name is Pete by the way."

He was a decent looking guy. I could tell he was very down to earth. We exchanged phone numbers and began to talk. During our many conversations, I received the news that he just got out of the army and became a cop.

One afternoon, he asked me if I wanted to chill. I replied, "Yes, I would like to go somewhere and get some ice cream."

He stated, "Ok. I'll pick you up in an hour."

We got ice cream and went by the water. We were enjoying the view and the conversation not realizing it was 4 AM. The conversation was going great. I had him laughing the whole night.

As we began to drive back to my house, I asked him if he smoked.

He replied, "No, I don't." Then he asked me if did.

I replied, "No. But I always wanted to try a cigar. Would you smoke one with me?"

He laughed and jokingly replied, "Are you serious?"

I look back at him and said, "Yeah, it's not like I'm asking you to do drugs with me. It's just a cigar. Relax."

He reluctantly gave in and said, "Ok. I will. I'm only doing it because you have a convincing way of talking."

We went around driving around, looking for a store that was open. We had no luck. But we found a gas station that had what we were looking for.

After we bought it, he said, "I can't believe I'm doing this with you. I've never smoked a day in my life."

I laughed and said, "Me, neither. So this will be a first date to remember."

We sat on the top of the trunk of his red car. I did the honor of lighting the cigar. I took a few pulls but I didn't know how to inhale the smoke. I decided to pass it to him. With his first pull, he started choking and his face turned red.

"I guess you inhaled it right," I told him. We both laughed.

He took me home at 6 AM. I enjoyed our first date. So did he.

He called me everyday. When I didn't answer, he would send me text messages. I liked the interest but it was a little too much for me. He never gave me the chance to call him.

One evening, we went to dinner and I noticed that he was getting really clingy. I didn't like the attention. It turned me off.

Anyway, he took me home. I said to myself, "Why is he parking in front of my house? I hope he doesn't think I'm inviting him in."

All of a sudden, he turned to look at me and said, "You are very funny. I love talking to you and enjoy your company. So since we are both single, would you like to be my girl?"

I was in a state of shock. This night just took a very awkward turn.

I looked at him and said, "It's only been three months since we began to talk and I don't want to rush into anything. Let's take it slow."

All the while I was saying this, I was thinking how I could rush myself out of the sticky and awkward situation. The only things that I wanted to go fast were my feet. I wanted to run out of the car and away from him.

He leaned over and gave me a hug and we both said our good nights. I went as so far to tell him that I had a headache. I told him I would call him later. Then, I reached for the car handle and pushed the door open.

He called me as soon as he got home. I guess he couldn't wait until later for me to call. I didn't answer my phone or respond to his the two paragraph text message he sent me. I was too busy thinking of ways to get rid of him.

Pete was a sweet guy. He was never rude or pushy. But I think he had issues or maybe I did. Who knows at this point?

He continued to call me back to back and send text messages. He would ask me how my day was going.

There is nothing wrong in a man asking me how my day is going but don't ask me every two hours. It started to get annoying. The more he did it. The more disinterested I got.

I decided to change my number. I thought this was a good idea as I wouldn't have to come face to face and explain myself to him. But, boy, oh boy, I was wrong.

Pete showed up at my house after a day of my phone number being changed. He said, "I was worried about you. What happened to your phone?"

I said, "Oh, I had to change my number. My ex keeps trying to get in contact with me. I was going to call you this evening to give you my new phone number, but since you are here, I'll go ahead and give it to you now."

I don't know how much longer I could keep lying to this guy. I wished I grew some balls already and told him how I really felt. I thought to myself if I pissed him off, he would be spiteful and give a whole bunch of tickets.

After thinking of all the possible excuses, I decided to use my ex-husband as an excuse.

I called him one evening. I said to him, "I'm calling to break some news to you. It may be bad for you. I decided to work on my marriage with my husband. I'm so sorry. But I'm still in love with my husband."

As expected, he did not handle the news very well. He continued to call me even after I told him what I was planning to do.

Once again, I changed my phone number. This was the end of Pete.

This situation with Pete caused me to come to a few conclusions. Here I had a guy with a good job, respectable, smart, and very into me. But all I wanted to do was get rid of him because he smothered me with all the attention he was giving me. Why didn't I feel the same way? Was I contradicting myself on what I really wanted? Maybe he just wasn't challenging enough for me. I wondered if I was going to regret the decision I made.

I had a conversation with a few friends and they told me I needed to take some time to focus on myself, enjoy the single life—because I never had the chance to be single. I wanted to go clubbing to feel that experience, so I did. I liked it so much that I started to party every weekend. Even on weekdays. This was all brand-new to me because I became a housewife and a mother at such a young age, that I never got the chance to hang out or party with any of my friends. I liked it a little too much, that it became my life. I met many different men. Some had wonderful personalities and some had no personalities.

I decided to start dating. I was curious to know how men thought and if all men were full of bull shit. This time I made sure I wasn't going to get attached or fall in love. This was all for experiment.

I got a part time job at my uncle's liquor store for some extra cash. One day at work, this guy came in and wanted to purchase alcohol. He looked very young, so I asked for ID, which of course he didn't have.

He said, "Ask your boss. I'm old enough. I come in here all the time."

My uncle said to me, "Go ahead and sell to him. He is old enough."

After that, I saw him in the store, but we never spoke to each other. One weekend, my girls and I decided to go clubbing. I got my drink and I did my usual, stand in the corner, talking to my friends. I looked up and saw this guy staring at me, but I couldn't make out the face, and then he waved. I waved back, not having a clue who he was. As the night went on, I started to dance. I felt someone grab my hands. When I looked up, there he was, the guy from my uncle's liquor store. He grabbed me close to his chest and started grinding on me. Oh, boy, he had some moves on the dance floor. Then he put my hands on his chest, which felt like a washboard. I knew what he trying to do. He wanted me to know he had an amazing body. I wasn't impressed.

After the dance, we exchanged names and phone numbers. His name was Rick. I had no intentions of calling him. He was not my type. Then again, I really didn't know what my type was. I guess I wasn't attracted to him, I should say. He called and messaged me a few times. I kept the conversation very short. He even asked me to hang out a few times, and invited me over to watch movies, but I never went.

Six months after that, I had a dream about him one night. So I sent him a message saying, "It was so funny you were in my dream last night."

He replied, "Let's make that dream a reality."

I laughed because I didn't mention what the dream was about. I dreamt he was scrubbing my kitchen floor, without a shirt. But I didn't tell him that.

He was very persistent about seeing me, so I finally gave him a chance, and invited him over for a New Year's drink that night. We drank, talked, and shared a few laughs. It was getting late, so I told him he could sleep on my couch, and he said okay.

The next day, I took him home, and we made plans to chill again. Since I was a single woman and hadn't had sex, I wondered if I had sex with him, would I catch feelings. I really needed to have sex. I turned to one of my friends who was experienced in these situations. Besides, we talked about it all the time.

So I asked her, "Is it even possible to sleep with someone you don't have feelings for?"

She said, "Yes, of course. If you just want sex and don't want any attachments, or any feelings, just leave right after sex. No hanging out, no cuddling, no talking after, or sharing personal information."

This sounded like a business proposition to me.

Well, one evening he invited me to come over to watch a movie. I said, "Okay."

This was my chance to sleep with him. That was all I could think about. Hey, it had been seven months since I had sex. Can you blame me?

So I went over and it happened. Oh, God, did I love it. The sex was so good that I forgot to leave right after. He called me every day after that to hang out. By hanging out, I meant having sex. I didn't have any feelings for him, even though we hung out after sex. I thought he was too into himself. He did a little modeling. I saw traces of selfishness. I also saw cockiness. It was always about him.

I could care less. I just wanted sex. The sex was amazing—the best I'd ever had.

One day I went over, and we had a stupid argument over a modeling picture he had taken. I guess he wasn't happy with my opinion which made me realize how sensitive he was.

I shook my head and said, "This is not going to work out," and left.

Two months later, I spoke to him. I saw it was his birthday on Facebook, so I sent him a happy birthday message. He messaged me back. He asked me if he could see me when he got back from Jamaica. I knew what he wanted. I wanted the same thing, too. Sex. Yes, we went back to having sex again. But this time, I left right after.

I continued my study on how to figure out men. At the time I was talking to seven other guys as my experiment. I had to figure out what really goes on in their heads. Apparently, more than I thought. So far, these seven guys all wanted different things. Some were looking for marriage. Some were looking for friends with benefits. I even met one guy who was living at home with his girlfriend and two kids, but had the balls to tell me that I needed to make up my mind if I wanted to be with him or not. He said he couldn't sit around and wait for me.

"The nerve of this asshole!" I said to myself.

It gets better. I met this other guy who told me, "I'm only into white girls, but for you I'll make an exception."

Oh, boy. How lucky am I.

These guys were all retarded. I felt sorry for the female who ended up with any of them.

I went to see Rick one night. I decided to turn him into my project. I'd been sleeping with him for a year now. Since I had no feelings for him, why not use him as my experiment? I started to study him. He was very into himself and loved attention from the ladies. Girls were crazy over him.

I thought to myself, "Why? Because he modeled?"

His attitude sucked. So did his sense of humor. Was I judging him a little too soon? For this, I decided to give him a chance to tell me more about himself. To do this, I had sex with him but didn't leave. I stayed around.

He said to me, "I'm surprised that you're still here."

I asked, "Why?"

He said, "Well, you leave right after we have sex, but I'm glad you decided to stay."

I couldn't help but laugh. We began to talk. He shared some pretty personal stuff with me that day. I was impressed to know he had a heart. So we began to spend more time together. I found myself cooking him dinner and spending the night over at his house. Sometimes he would stay at my house. I still had no feelings for him.

One evening, he asked me to have dinner with his family. It was a very big deal for him and he wanted me to be a part of that. He was reuniting with his two brothers for the first time in a long time and wanted me there. I was honored but confused. Why me?

When I got to the restaurant, he held my hands. He called me baby every time he asked me a question, and kept kissing me the entire night. I'm not going to lie. I liked the attention he was giving me. He even told his brother he was happy I was back in his life. Wow. My head was spinning. What was going on here?

"Are we a couple?" I was thinking in my head. I wasn't aware of it if we were. Anyway, I was starting to like this guy now. He paid me all the attention I needed, answered all my calls, and never stood me up. He introduced me to his friends and family. I felt as if I were a part of his life. I knew there was something up with this guy. I couldn't put my finger on it, though.

Two weeks later, he told me he had gone on a date. I was in shock. I thought he was into me. I thought everything was going well.

I said out loud, "What? You were on a date?"

He said, "Yes. We are going out again."

I was jealous, and I said, "No, you're not. You're not going to date anyone while you're sleeping with me."

He asked, "But we are just friends, right? You never told me how you felt about me."

So I said to him, "I care about you a lot, and I think you should give us a chance."

Now here comes the bullshit.

He said, "Nadia, I really like you, but I can't give you what you want right now."

What the fuck was going on? Was I experimenting on him or was he experimenting on me? This guy had just flipped the entire script on me. Confusing as the situation was, I had to leave after he said that. This wasn't making sense to me, so why stick around? I asked him not to reach out to me. I left thinking to myself that at least I had taken a shot at love. I said love, because I was starting to fall for him. After being around someone for a year and spending so much time together, it's only a matter of time before you fall in love. Trust me. I'll never put myself out there like that again. Rejection doesn't feel so nice.

I needed to know if there was any possibility for our being together. Things, however, didn't turn out the way I'd hoped, so my conclusion was to walk away. I couldn't afford to get hurt anymore.

One month after my rejection, I was on Facebook. I saw he had posted that his grandmother had passed away. I knew how close he was to his grandmother because he was always talking about her. I think I watched at least twenty videos that he recorded of the two of them spending time together.

I sent him a message that night saying that I was very sorry about his loss as I read about it on Facebook. I offered my help if he ever needed anything. I was there for him.

He responded, "Can you come over?"

I said, "Yes."

I went over to comfort him and have sex. Don't judge me. I have needs. He was as happy to see me as I was to see him and the sexual attraction was flying all over the room. I wanted him as badly as he wanted me, sexually I should say. I remember that night. Once again, it was tremendous sex. I think he felt it too.

After sex that night, we started talking again.

He said to me, "I'm not seeing the girl I told you about before. I totally downgraded when I left you for her. Her fake hair turned me off."

I laughed, saying in my head, "I got him back."

He had to leave to attend to his grandmother's funeral, but we stayed in contact with each other every day. He even texted me at 3 AM saying that he missed me. I was falling into his trap once again.

When he came back home, I picked him up at the airport.

He grabbed me and hugged me so tightly, and said, "You have no idea how happy I am to see you."

The following week was my birthday. I was having everyone over to my house for drinks and dinner. He told me he wasn't going to work that day. He wanted to spend my birthday with me. Everyone came over. We were all having a great time. Did I forget to mention that I invited some other guys over as well? Well, yeah I did.

One happened to be the back-up guy. The others? Just friends. Rick did not see it this way. The entire night his eyes were glued to me. He watched my every move, even if I sneaked off with another guy. I couldn't shake him. A part of me was happy. He was jealous. Serves him right. He rejected me. Now, he gets a taste of his medicine.

My friends knew the deal. They distracted both guys.

After some time, to make his presence known, he decided to sing, "Can I hit it in the morninggggg . . ." and grabbed and kissed me.

Of course, you could say, the back-up guy was in shock.

He soon left after this, saying in private to me, "We are going to have a conversation about this later."

I didn't really care. I had Rick.

He stayed the night.

The next day was Thanksgiving. We woke up and had breakfast together before I took him home. I was flying out that night to Barbados to celebrate my birthday weekend with my cousins.

He texted me when I boarded the plane and said, "I miss you already. Call me as soon as you get back."

I missed him too and couldn't wait to come back.

I got back. Everything was going great. We didn't go one night without sleeping next to each other. A few days before Christmas, he said that he was going to spend Christmas with his ex-girlfriend.

I asked, "Why?" This troubled me greatly. It completely upset my plans for Christmas.

He said for the past four years, he'd spent Christmas there because they treated him like family.

"Besides," he said, "They bought my ticket already."

What could I possibly say about this situation except that it didn't make sense to me.

Anyway, he left. I was pretty upset about it. He texted me. I didn't respond. This is when it got crazy. I didn't hear from him on Christmas Day. I didn't bother to call, either. Four days after, I called him. I told him that we needed to talk. He said to come over.

When I got there, I asked him, "Did you sleep with her?"

He looked me in the eyes and said, "No."

My second question was, "Why didn't you call me for Christmas?"

He responded, "I did." (Which was a lie.)

Before I could have said anything else, he started kissing me and taking my clothes off. I knew what was about to happen. I also wanted it to happen . . . even though I knew he was lying. I decided to leave the topic alone. We went to bed. The next day, he told me some friends were flying in to celebrate New Year's with him. He wanted me to meet them. This was the night before New Year's.

We picked up his friends from the airport and went back to his house to get dressed. We all decided to go dancing.

His friends asked me, "What are you doing for the New Year?"

I said, "I'm staying home. A few of my friends are coming over."

They said to me, "Come join us in Times Square."

I said, "I really can't. I made plans already."

I looked at Rick that night, because he was acting very weird. He was ignoring me the entire night. We got home about five in the morning. I went to sleep for an hour at his house.

I woke up. I gave him a kiss. I said, "You should be breaking in the New Year with me. And who are you going to kiss when the ball drops?"

He said, "Well not those two for sure," meaning his two boys. I laughed.

I left so I could start getting prepared for the party I was having. Around seven in the evening, I called him to say, "Be safe in Times Square, and have fun."

He didn't answer. He always answered my calls or texted me right back. This time I got no response. Not even at midnight. No happy New Year call or text. Something didn't feel right. I went on Facebook around 3 AM. There it was: a picture of him and his so-called ex-girlfriend, celebrating New Year's together. It's funny. I didn't see this on his page. I saw it on his friend's page. This was one of the two guys I'd picked up from the airport. Apparently, she had been taking pictures all over his house. His friends seemed to like her very much as well . . . because there were quite a few pictures posted of both her alone and with Rick.

After I saw the picture, I called him right away. My blood was boiling. I think if I'd seen him that night, I would've set his balls on fire. He didn't answer my phone call. I sent him a two-paragraph text message, letting him know I found out everything. By everything, I mean everything. This is why I never found out about his ex-girlfriend.

He had two Facebook pages. She was on one. I was on the other. Since she lived two-and-a-half hours away, he led me to believe that was the reason they weren't together. They were having a long-distance relationship and spent every special event together. It's crazy how much you can find out on Facebook without leaving your home. He deleted me off Facebook within three minutes after getting my texts, and never responded to any of my messages. I guess that was the guilty sign.

I was devastated over this situation. Here I was once again with a broken heart, thinking, "How can he sleep in my bed every night, introduce me to his friends and family, and then do this?"

I guess I'd been the second chick all this time. He'd used me to fill in the empty space because his girlfriend wasn't able to.

When we fall in love, we don't pay attention to little details. My first sign was him going to spend Christmas with his ex-girlfriend. If you're starting something new with someone, you have to let go of your past. Obviously, he didn't. His past was his present. I wanted to give him the benefit of the doubt that maybe he was really good friends with his ex, but once again, I was wrong.

I guess I got what I deserved. I was seeing another guy while with Rick, but for security purposes only. You guys met him in the description of my party. He was the one who left, upset with me. Now, you know that women can be just as deceiving as men. The question is, who is more deceitful, men or women? We all have our own opinions on that, but in my book, men will always be number one when it comes to being deceitful.

Now, here comes the story of the back-up guy, Danny. I've known him about five years now. We used to work together. I always had a crush on him. I kept him around because he had some good qualities that Rick didn't have. I wanted both of them. I guess I wanted to have my cake and eat it, too. Danny and I bonded on a different level. It wasn't sexual like Rick . . . but I'm not saying we didn't have sex. We had great conversations. There was never a dull moment. He always had me laughing. We fought like two five-year-olds. The question I ask myself is: If I really had to choose between Danny and Rick, who would have been my first pick?

Unfortunately, this wasn't the case. I never got to choose. Now Rick is gone. I let go of Danny as well. I felt as if he didn't have everything I was looking for, so why keep him around? I didn't want to be selfish anymore, or hurt him. My heart really did belong to Rick. I couldn't force myself to love Danny. The feelings just weren't there.

I still want Rick. I will do what I need to do in order to get him back. I will not lose faith as I'm pretty persistent in getting what I want, no, need, to be happy.

Now, here comes the part I've been dying to tell you.

I would like to tell you the results of my experiment. What we as females don't pay attention to in men. We as females don't pay attention to small details, like I did with Rick. For instance, pay attention to the way your man talks. What topic does he always talk about? Pay attention to the friends he hangs out with. What are their characters like?

Pay attention to your man's body language. This also tells a lot.

Ladies, you can't read a man through sex. Men are always horny. They don't even have to be physically attracted to you to sleep with you. Men are always seeking a challenge. Sleeping with them too soon is showing that you are weak. Don't expect a long-term commitment. If a man keeps coming back for more sex, that doesn't mean he is starting to fall in love with you. He is just doing what you allow him to do. What man would say no to sex?

I'm not saying all men cheat. I'll tell you that the majority of them do. If a guy knows he looks good, and is capable of getting any girl he wants, then he will use it to his advantage. Some men cheat for financial purposes, especially if the female is willing to take care of him. Some do it because of insecurity problems. Other men cheat just to maintain their status of being the man. It's also an ego thing.

I learned this from experience: Don't spend your time trying to change a man or make him fall in love with you. At the end, when he does fall in love, you will fall out of love with him.

I know most of you females will agree with me on this: The two things I learned that can make a man run for the hills, is "I love you," and "I'm pregnant." Men can't handle these two things very well because they don't like to feel trapped. Don't ever tell a man you love him first, or show signs that you are falling in love with him. By signs, I mean things like buying him certain clothes because you think he'll look cute in them . . . cooking him dinner, offering to do his laundry. All I'm saying is that you can show him you care but know your limits.

It is okay to say no sometimes. This might even work in your favor. Always remember, a man doesn't like to be rejected in any way whatsoever. We as females have the idea in our heads that if we say no, men will think we're not capable of being the perfect women they want.

How can you tell if a man is really into you? Some people say, if he listens to you. Well, this is not necessarily true in my opinion. Men already know this. Some men use it to their advantage. Always remember: Some men are good at pretending. Don't get caught up if he remembers your birthday or your last name. I think if a guy really likes you, he will try to impress you. He will call to say hello or ask how your day is going. He will offer to assist you in any problems without you having to even ask for help. If he comes around you and you are not looking your very best and still finds you beautiful, then this is all the sign you need.

Let's talk about age. Does age play an important part in a relationship?

I'm going to speak from experience on this one. I try to stay in my age range when I date. I've dated a few older guys because they say the older the man, the more mature and experienced he is. Well, I've got news for you, ladies. This is not true. I dated a 25 year old and a 34 year old and I couldn't tell the difference. I think it varies with the man and also how he was brought up as a kid. Never think the older the man, the less likely he would be to cheat because you will be in for a shock and a surprise.

Let me tell you what scares us ladies when we turn thirty.

One, our biological clock is ticking. We are being pressured by our family to get married and have kids. We are scared of ending up alone. Will we ever find love?

Well, this is all bullshit to me. This is how I view life. Thirty is young. Don't rush into anything unless you are 100% sure of it. If you ever have to question a situation and use the words "if" and "but," then that wasn't for you. Take marriage for instance. I think it's overrated, speaking from my experience. A piece of paper sure as hell doesn't stop a man from cheating. The older we grow, the more knowledge we gain. The more knowledge we gain, the better decisions we make. Don't ever rush to live. You may be missing out on the best years of your life.

I want to sum my life up for you guys.

After nine years I finally reunited with my father. He got to meet his granddaughter for the first time. My dad is still living in Guyana. He is now remarried and has two sons of his own. Seeing my father was one of the happiest days of my life. I don't hold him responsible for anything that he did to me. Leaving me alone in America made me the woman I am today. I always wanted to make my father proud of me. I didn't turn out to be the perfect daughter he expected or wanted to be. But I got something better than that; I gained his respect. This is more than I could ask for.

Now, my father and I are inseparable. I can't go a week without talking to him. I can talk to him about everything and anything. I'm surprised to see how much of a changed man he is. He stopped drinking and his wife told me he's never laid hands on her. They look very happy together, but I know in my heart that he still loves my mom.

Speaking of my mother, she is still living in Canada. She has also remarried and has no kids. She finally found her happiness and freedom. The last time I spoke to her, she was going to school to learn how to read and write. I'm so proud of her.

As for my brother Richard, he got divorced after a few months of being married because he was abusive to his wife. Now he is living all alone. He hardly keeps in touch with any of us.

As for me, after living in America nineteen years without my legal documents, I was happy to finally become a citizen. Now, I travel the world with my daughter in hope that one day I'll meet my Romeo and fall in love. As for my days of struggle, they're finally over—but I wouldn't go back and change a thing. Life doesn't faze me anymore. It respects me now that I have grown.

As the days pass by, our quest for love will always live on, as our hearts desire and mourn for it. We will always suffer the heartbreak, but that will never stop us from loving again, as it will come to us as if we were in love for the first time.